L I F E W A Y S

The Ojibwe

R A Y M O N D   B I A L

BENCHMARK BOOKS

MARSHALL CAVENDISH
NEW YORK

SERIES CONSULTANT: JOHN BIERHORST

ACKNOWLEDGMENTS

This book would not have been possible without the generous help of a number of individuals and organizations that have devoted themselves to preserving the culture of the Ojibwe. I would like to thank the staffs of the Mille Lacs Indian Museum and Mille Lacs Kathio State Park for their generous help with this book, including permission to make photographs at these wonderful sites. I would also like to acknowledge the assistance of the Minnesota Historical Society, the National Archives, the Library of Congress, and the Philbrook Museum for providing a number of illustrations.

I am very much indebted to my editor, Kate Nunn, and to Doug Sanders for guiding this book through to completion and to John Bierhost for his careful review of the manuscript. I would like to thank my wife, Linda, and my children Anna, Sarah, and Luke who accompanied me to the forests and lakes of Minnesota to make photographs for this book.

5231 0778

Library of Congress Cataloging-in-Publication Data
Bial, Raymond.
The Ojibwe / Raymond Bial.
p. cm. — (Lifeways)
Includes bibliographical references and index.
Summary: Discusses the history, culture, social structure, beliefs, and customs of the Ojibwe Indians.
ISBN 0-7614-0863-0
1. Ojibwe Indians—History—Juvenile literature. 2. Ojibwe Indians—Social life and customs—Juvenile literature. [1. Ojibwe Indians. 2. Indians of North America.] I. Title.
II. Series: Bial, Raymond. Lifeways.
E99.C6B53 2000 977'.004973—dc21 99-12202 CIP
Printed in Italy
6 5

Cover photographs: Raymond Bial

The photographs in this book are used by permission and through the courtesy of:
The Philbrook Museum of Art, Tulsa, Oklahoma: 1, 51, 88. Raymond Bial: 6, 8-9, 12, 17, 18, 20-21, 25, 26, 32-33, 42, 44, 47, 60, 61, 70-71, 74, 76, 77, 78, 90-91, 92-93, 96, 98-99. Minnesota Historical Society: 23, 28-29, 30, 37, 38, 48, 53, 55, 59, 64, 80-81, 84, 95, 102, 103, 105, 107, 110, 111, 112. National Archive: 109.

This book is respectfully dedicated
to all the people who have worked to
keep alive the flame of traditional
life among the Ojibwe.

Contents

Author's Note

At THE DAWN OF THE TWENTIETH CENTURY, NATIVE Americans were thought to be a vanishing race. However, despite four hundred years of warfare, deprivation, and disease, American Indians have not gone away. Countless thousands have lost their lives, but over the course of this century the populations of native tribes have grown tremendously. Even as American Indians struggle to adapt to modern Western life, they have also kept the flame of their traditions alive—the language, religion, stories, and the everyday ways of life. An exhilarating renaissance in Native American culture is now sweeping the nation from coast to coast.

The Lifeways books depict the social and cultural life of the major nations, from the early history of native peoples in North America to their present-day struggles for survival and dignity. Historical and contemporary photographs of traditional subjects, as well as period illustrations, are blended throughout each book so that readers may gain a sense of family life in a tipi, a hogan, or a longhouse.

No single book can comprehensively portray the intricate and varied lifeways of an entire tribe, or nation. I only hope that young people will come away with a deeper appreciation for the rich tapestry of Indian culture—both then and now—and a keen desire to learn more about these first Americans.

1. Origins

For hundreds of years, the Ojibwe have made their home beside the lakes and streams of the North. Here, the sun rises over Mille Lacs, one of the largest lakes in northern Minnesota.

MAKING THEIR HOMES IN THE NORTHERN REACHES WHERE THE WINTERS are bitterly cold and game is scarce in the coldest months, the Ojibwe have long called upon spirits to guide them through times of peril. The foremost spirit, or manitou, is the legendary Nanabozho, who helped the people survive in the wilderness and to understand their place in the universe. Nanabozho brought many helpful tools and skills to the Ojibwe. From him, they learned to make birch bark canoes, snowshoes, and bows and arrows. Nanabozho also taught the Ojibwe to harvest wild rice and tap maple trees for their sweet sap.

Here is the story of Nanabozho, sometimes called Manabozho or Winabojo, and how he came to help the people.

"The Birth of Nanabozho"

The daughter of the moon, living in the sky world, had not been married long when another woman, a jealous rival, lured her to a grapevine swing on the banks of a lake. The rival encouraged her to hold onto the swing, then pushed her out over the water. When she reached the center of the water, she fell through the water to the earth below.

She had been expecting a child, and when she reached the earth she gave birth to a baby girl. As the little girl began to grow, the mother warned her to be careful of the west wind. She must never stoop to expose herself to its great force.

One day the young daughter, now grown, forgot the warning and the ice-cold west wind swept into her clothing and killed her.

Next to her body at the place where she had died, her mother found a tiny infant. She tenderly nursed the infant and in time he grew into the strong and handsome Nanabozho.

Very little is known of Nanabozho as he grew up with his grandmother. From an early age he did have great and varied powers, but he did not make use of them. He was simply too timid and filled with youthful innocence to show off his miraculous abilities. Yet, as he rose to manhood, he began to demonstrate his remarkable strength, wisdom, and courage, as well as great cunning and perseverance. In knowledge and intelligence he was far superior to all others. Because of his innocence he was occasionally the object of ridicule. Yet it became clear that he was a manitou, or spirit, as well as a man with magical powers. He could talk with the animals, including reptiles, birds, and fish, and transform himself into any animal he pleased. Considering himself related to these living creatures, he referred to them as "my brothers."

Both human and supernatural, Nanabozho possesses all the powers and virtues admired and needed by the people. Among the many spirits in their world, he has helped the Ojibwe to feed, clothe, and shelter themselves. He is their greatest hero, the personification of the triumph of good over evil, and guides them along the right path through life.

THOUSANDS OF YEARS AGO, THE ANCESTORS OF THE OJIBWE, ALONG WITH other Native Americans, journeyed over a strip of land that once connected Siberia and Alaska. Following the herds of shaggy bison and other wild animals, they spread south and eastward

The Ojibwe once paddled their birch bark canoes over the rough waters of northern lakes, trading with the French voyageurs and scouting prime spots for hunting and trapping.

over the continent of North America. Also known as the Chippewa and the Anishinabe, the Ojibwe (oh-JIB-way, sometimes spelled Ojibwa or Ojibway) eventually settled in the northern Great Lakes region over five hundred years ago.

No one is sure of the definition—or even the source—of the word *Ojibwe*. It may refer to something puckered up, such as the style of Ojibwe moccasins, which were sewn together at the top. Or the word may be a version of "o-jib-i-weg," which means "those who make pictographs." The term *Chippewa*, which comes from a slight mispronunciation of the name, was often used on treaties and other government documents. Ojibwe has been increasingly favored in recent years, although many Ojibwe prefer to be known as Anishinabe, which means "original people" in their language. The Ojibwe language is actually a group of several closely related languages, which belong to the great Algonquian group, or family, of over thirty languages spoken in northern North America from the Atlantic coast to the Rocky Mountains. Many Native American tribes speak Algonquian languages, including the Arapaho, Cheyenne, Blackfoot, Fox, Shawnee, Abenaki, and Delaware.

According to oral history, the people once lived to the east, near the sea, "on the shores of the great salt water, toward the rising sun." This place may have been the Atlantic Ocean near the mouth of the St. Lawrence River, or possibly Hudson Bay in the north of Canada. Little is known about their early history in this land of rivers and lakes, except that the people gradually moved westward. It is not known why they moved from the Northeast. During this migration, which spanned several hundred years, they suffered great hardship. It is said that when the people reached Saint Marys River and the Straits of Mackinac, where Lakes Huron, Michigan, and Superior nearly touch each other, they separated into three tribes—the Potawatomi, Ottawa, and Ojibwe. The three tribes entered into an alliance known as the Three Fires Confederacy, or the Council of Three Tribes. The Ojibwe were considered the oldest brother of this alliance, the Ottawa the next oldest brother, and the Potawatomi the youngest.

Eventually, the Ojibwe spread over a vast territory that arced from the northeastern plains of present-day North Dakota across northern Minnesota, Wisconsin, and Michigan to the forested region just east of Lake Superior and Lake Huron. Their land extended northward into present-day Canada, from central Saskatchewan to southern Ontario. Although primarily a people of the forest, some Ojibwes adopted the lifestyle of the Plains Indians after moving onto the prairies of Saskatchewan and North Dakota. To the Ojibwe, this land was given to them by *Kitche Manitou*, the Great Spirit, and it belonged to everyone in the tribe.

Much of this region was shared with other tribes, yet the Ojibwe became the dominant people and, over time, one of the largest Native American tribes. Their sprawling lands abounded with wildlife and were rich with timber and copper. They became the most prominent of native traders with the French in the upper

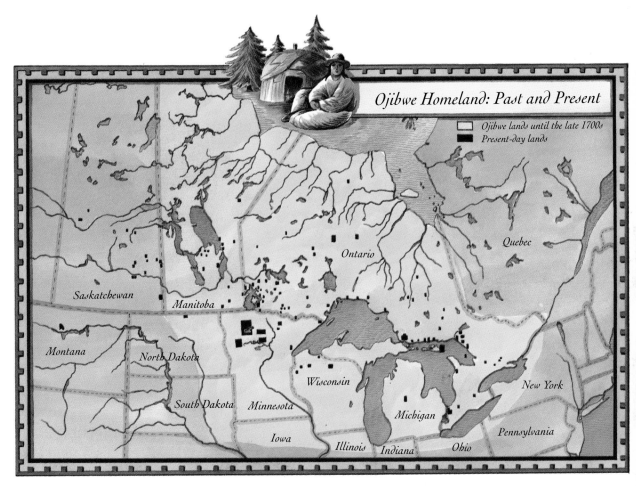

Ojibwe Homeland: Past and Present

☐ Ojibwe lands until the late 1700s
■ Present-day lands

Saskatchewan

Manitoba

Ontario

Quebec

Montana

North Dakota

South Dakota

Minnesota

Wisconsin

Michigan

New York

Iowa

Illinois

Indiana

Ohio

Pennsylvania

This map shows the northern homelands of the Ojibwe. Historically, the Ojibwe dominated the region around the Great Lakes. Today, many Ojibwe live on reservations in the United States and on reserves in Canada.

Great Lakes. However, from the moment they first came into contact with Europeans—French explorers, traders, and missionaries in the seventeenth century—the lives of the people began to change.

The People and the Land

For hundreds of years the Ojibwe lived among lakes and marshes, sheltered by the hardwoods of the eastern forest—maple, elm, oak, hickory, chestnut, and beech—which extended from Ohio to the Mississippi River. The canopy of trees reached northward, giving way to stands of white birch and coniferous forests of white pine, jack pine, and white spruce. Scattered among the evergreens were poplar and aspen trees while tamarack, black spruce, and white cedar grew in the many bogs and swamps of the northern forests. The birch tree, which provided white bark for wigwams and canoes, as well as household goods, had sacred meaning. Birches stood at the very heart of Ojibwe life; people were careful to peel the supple bark without harming the living trees.

The north country abounded in wildlife: the bear, deer, wolf, coyote, fox, wolverine, and lynx. There were also beavers, otters, muskrats, porcupines, raccoons, fishers, woodchucks, rabbits, weasels, and mink, all of which the Ojibwe hunted or trapped. The marshes and lakes teemed with fish and fowl, especially ducks and geese—the flocks often so large they blackened the skies. The Ojibwe hunted deer for their meat and hides, but they favored the greasy flesh of the bear. They could trap just about any animal, but came to rely on providing beaver pelts to the French in what became an international trade.

There were no high mountains and scarcely any hills in these forests. Here, glaciers had long ago scoured out basins for the thousands of ponds and lakes that dotted the blanket of green trees. Rivers and streams wound through the north woods, forming a vast network among these small bodies of water and joining them to Lakes Superior, Michigan, and Huron. The Ojibwe pad-

A mong the stands of dark evergreens are graceful birch trees, growing in clumps or jagged rows at the edge of the forest. The Ojibwe use the bark to make not only canoes but many household goods.

*T*all grasses line the shores of many of the region's lakes. Of these, wild rice is the most important to the Ojibwe. They paddle among the wispy stalks, bend the stems over, and knock the seeds into their canoes.

dled their swift canoes down rivers, and along the banks of the Great Lakes to trade wild rice, corn, and animal pelts with their allies, notably the French, and to wage war on their enemies. From Europeans they acquired firearms, and with this decisive weapon in the hands of their warriors, the Ojibwe expanded westward in the late eighteenth and early nineteenth centuries.

Like other American Indians, the Ojibwe lived according to the cycle of the seasons. In the spring, the sap flowed, and like delicate green lace the buds emerged on the trees. They tapped the maple trees and boiled down the sap to make crumbly brown maple sugar. When the soil thawed and was warmed by the sun, they dug with sticks and planted corn, beans, and squash. In early summer, Juneberries, wild strawberries, raspberries, and cherries were gathered before the long, dry months of July and August, when the ears of corn ripened on the stalks, and blueberries dotted the forest floor.

Come autumn, the trees became a splendor of brilliant red, yellow, and orange leaves. Corn leaves and stalks faded to tan, pumpkins glowed orange against the damp ground, and drying beans rattled in their shells. Women harvested these crops and then paddled in canoes onto lakes and marshes to gather wild rice, before the first cold winds swept down upon them. Throughout the long winter, the pines rose in jagged silhouettes against the purple sky at the end of the day, and the snows collected in the valleys and blanketed clearings in the forest. Frozen over, rivers and lakes disappeared under the drifts, and people settled around the fire, trudging only short distances in their snowshoes in search of a rabbit or deer. Game was scarce through the hard winters, and many would have starved without the stores of wild rice, dried meat, and corn.

Whatever the time of year, people provided for themselves from the forests and fields with little harm to the wilderness that surrounded them. To the Ojibwe, the land was filled with many spirits to whom they gave thanks. The earth belonged to no one and to everyone. It was the home of their ancestors, the place where they now lived, and the land they hoped would sustain their children and grandchildren long into the future.

2.Bands

The Ojibwe lived in wigwams made of saplings lashed together and covered with sheets of birch bark or reed mats. These practical buildings could be easily set up in the woods.

ALTHOUGH THE OJIBWE SPOKE CLOSELY RELATED LANGUAGES AND HAD many customs in common, they did not unite themselves around a central government. Instead, they chose to live in seminomadic bands. Made up of several families, the bands included parents, unmarried children, and sometimes grandparents. Each band had its own leaders who were selected not through heredity, but because of their wisdom, leadership abilities, and genuine concern for the well-being of the people. Moving from one camp to another—depending on the kind of food available during that season—the bands sustained themselves by hunting, fishing, and gathering wild plants. In the early spring, several bands came together in maple sugar camps. From summer through autumn, they camped along rivers to plant crops and to fish in the lively waters, then moved on to harvest the rice lakes. However, during the autumn hunt and the deep snows of winter, the bands scattered in smaller, more isolated camps spread throughout the northern wilderness.

Clans

Each person in an Ojibwe band was born into a clan, a kind of extended family, named for a bird, fish, or mammal. The clan animal, or totem, represented the creature believed to be the original ancestor. The word *totem* is drawn from the Ojibwe term *ototeman*, which indicates belonging, or being related, to one's kin. At one time there were more than twenty clans, named after the animals that lived in the Ojibwe homeland. Among the clans that

*A*mong the Ojibwe, men headed families and clans, each of which was represented by a totem, or clan animal. People also traced their family history through their father's lines.

thrive today are the Catfish, Sturgeon, Pike, Whitefish, and Sucker. There are also the Eagle, Crane, Loon, and Goose, as well as the Reindeer, Marten, Moose, and Bear.

The Ojibwe were patrilineal, meaning family descent, including clan membership, was traced through the father's side of the family. People were not allowed to marry within their own clan.

When a couple married, they often lived with the wife's family, at least for a few years. The men might be family and band leaders, while the women prepared and served the food, and managed the wigwam. The household often included grandparents, in addition to the husband and children, all of whom knew their place within the dwelling.

Each clan within the band had specialized tasks. Certain clans governed the band. Some made birch bark canoes, while others tended cornfields or gathered wood. The Ojibwe worked together to insure the well-being of everyone in the band. Much of the work of providing food, clothing, and shelter required that people cooperate and care about each other. Whenever two men went hunting together they always asked about each member of the other's family. Sharing was also important—anyone lucky enough to acquire a little extra food was expected to share his good fortune with others in his band or even in other villages. Generosity was never forgotten, and when able, even years later, a person repaid kindness with a gift. A strong sense of community was necessary if the people were going to survive in the cold reaches of the northern wilderness.

Wigwams

Depending on the season or activity, the Ojibwe lived in different types of homes, including the peaked lodge, the bark house, and the tipi. However, the most common was the wigwam, which means "home" or "dwelling." This round or oval-shaped

*T*his photograph shows the dome-shaped structure of the wigwam. Supple branches were stuck into the ground, bent over, and lashed together. The resulting frame was light but very strong.

house usually measured about ten to twelve feet in diameter. Often built on a slope so rainwater would drain away, the wigwam consisted of a frame of long poles, bent in the shape of a dome. Women used leather strips or twine made from the inner bark of basswood to lash the poles together. The frame was then covered

Snow often drifted high up the sides of the wigwam during the most brutal winter months. But, whatever the season, the wigwam kept the Ojibwe dry and provided shelter from the elements.

with overlapping sheets of birch bark or cattail mats. A hole left for a doorway was covered by a leather flap in cold weather. A fire was kept burning in the center of the bare floor, smoke twining up through a small smoke hole left in the roof. When the people moved on again, the wigwam could be taken down quickly; the birch bark or the mats were rolled up and easily carried to the next campsite.

Although wigwams were relatively simple to make and set up, they kept their inhabitants dry during the summer rains and warm during the bitterly cold winters. Women wove bulrush mats and hung them on the inside walls of the wigwam as a buffer against the chill wind. They also placed mats for sitting and sleeping on the earthen floor. Family members had their own place around the fire—the parents on either side of the entrance, daughters next to their mother, and sons next to their father.

The Ojibwe used bearskins, deer hides, and blankets for bedding. Some made pillows and thin beds of hide or cloth filled with duck feathers. They spread cedar boughs on the ground, which they covered with mats, and then the bedding. During the day, they rolled up their bedding and used it as a seat or stored it along the inside walls of the wigwam. During the evenings, especially through the long winters, the fire burned brightly as old people told stories, women made fishnets or birch bark bowls, and the men repaired snowshoes and traps. Food was stored within the wigwam or in a small log or bark storehouse located nearby. It was also hung from a high rack or frame next to the wigwam.

Like the Sioux, Cheyenne, and other Plains Indians, the Ojibwe made tipis. However, the Ojibwe used them only as temporary shelters, usually during hunting trips.

Women took pride in their work around the wigwam–preparing meals and making clothes, as well as storing wild rice and maple sugar. Here, a woman stands with quiet dignity.

Occasionally, people lived in peaked lodges that resembled A-frames. Two sets of angled poles were lashed against a ridgepole and covered with birch bark or cattail mats. There was an entrance at each end. Sometimes, people built extended bark lodges, like the longhouses of the Iroquois to the east, or they made their homes in skin-covered tipis like the Sioux and Cheyenne to the west. Sometimes, during warm weather people slept outside. The village also included a sweat lodge for purification and healing rituals, and a small wigwam in which women secluded themselves during menstruation.

When they journeyed away from camp to hunt, trade, or trap, men occasionally set up temporary cone-shaped shelters, which were made of branches and resembled small tipis.

3.Lifeways

Women made storage containers from birch bark, using both the white outer and brown inner bark. Today, many women continue to honor their heritage by making baskets and bowls.

THE OJIBWE HAVE LONG THOUGHT OF THEMSELVES AS LIVING IN UNION, as one, not only with animals and plants, but with the earth, the sun, the moon, and the stars. People still strive to live in harmony with all the creations of the Great Spirit. They believe that people must know how to walk properly upon the earth. This knowledge, which is the source of their identity, is carried deep within their hearts. And it must be passed from one generation to another, if the people are to understand themselves and their place in the world.

So, the stories, along with their life lessons, are remembered and shared whenever an old man speaks to the children or a mother sings to the baby in her arms. With no written language, the Ojibwe speak through these stories and memories, along with the messages imparted in the names of their families, clans, and bands. It is how the people come to understand the mystery of birth, the complexity of growing up, and the acceptance of old age and death.

Cycle of Life

The Ojibwe were closely bound to the land and the changing seasons, as well as the mysteries of life—the cycle of birth, growth, and death in the generations of plants, animals, and people. Their life revolved around the daily tasks of raising children and preparing meals, and the seasonal activities of hunting, fishing, trapping, and the gathering of wild rice.

Birth. Couples did not have large families—usually there were only about two children in each family.

Whenever a baby was born, there was noisy rejoicing. It was believed that a baby who came into a rowdy world would grow up to be very brave. The men of the father's family symbolically wrestled with the men of another family for possession of the baby. The leader of the "winning" family carried the baby four times around the fire as the people sang, "We have caught the little bird."

Babies spent their first year strapped to a cradleboard. About two feet long and ten inches wide, this cedar board had a foot brace at the bottom and a hickory hoop at the top to protect the baby's head. The mother placed her baby on a bedding of sphagnum moss that also served as a diaper. She then bound the baby to the board with cloth or buckskin wrappers embroidered with beads in striking floral patterns.

The cradleboard helped keep the baby's back straight, which was important to the Ojibwe. Bundled up, the baby also felt comfortable and cozy. The mother slung the cradleboard to her back and carried her baby wherever she traveled. Or she propped the cradleboard against the wall as she cooked within the wigwam, or rested it against a tree as she worked outside, tending cornfields or tanning deer hides. Whatever she was doing, the young one could watch her.

From the cradleboard hoop dangled toys to amuse the infant and charms to protect it. The baby's moccasins also had holes cut into the soles. If called back to the land of the dead, the baby could inform the spirits that his moccasins were in no condition for the journey.

Several times each day mothers took their babies out of the cradleboard for changing and a little exercise. Mothers were loving and devoted to their babies. They nursed them for about ten months, after which they were weaned onto a broth made from wild rice flavored with meat or fish.

Childhood. As they grew up, children received as many as six different names. Given to the baby not long after birth, the first was revealed to a "namer" in a dream. Another name was given by the parents, then a nickname by someone else in the family or clan. Others came from the child's kinship or clan name, and a name might come from a vision quest. In later times, people might also be known by the English translation of their names.

From the time they were babies, children learned to be quiet—crying could alert an enemy to one's whereabouts. Children were also taught to learn by listening, especially when an elder was speaking. Parents were loving and gentle to their children, who were taught to respect others. Because of the perilously cold winters, they carefully tended their little ones. They rarely punished their children, although they might frighten them by placing a scarecrow where it was unsafe to play. Or a masked man might chase the children until they ran home, if they would not stop playing in the evenings.

*W*omen kept their babies safely tucked in cradleboards. Even today some women continue to carry their infants in this traditional way.

The Ojibwe welcomed babies into their lives and cherished their children. Here, a woman from Mille Lacs, Minnesota, carries her infant on her back. The baby is swaddled in a blanket for warmth against the winter winds.

During the summer children played outside, but in the winter they had to be amused inside the wigwam. If they did not behave themselves, their mother might tell them, "Keep still or the owl will get you." If they would not obey, she held back the door flap and called out into the night, "Come in, owl. Come and get these children who will not keep still." The children hid under the bedding and were soon fast asleep. Other mothers might say a bear claw or a ghost's leg would get them, but these warnings proved too scary for some. So, the owl became the wild creature of choice in stories. He scared the children enough to make them go to sleep, but not so much that they would have bad dreams.

Parents emphasized practical training for their children. Girls were very close to their mothers, learning how to take care of the household, harvest wild rice, make maple sugar, and fashion birch bark rolls. A mother might caution her daughter, "You must not grow up to live outdoors and be made fun of because you do not know how to make a good wigwam." Fathers were responsible for teaching their sons. Boys became skilled with the bow and arrow in preparation for hunting and warfare. They also made and paddled canoes, set beaver traps, and learned the ways of the woods and water.

Coming-of-Age. When a girl had her first period, or "moon time," she had to isolate herself in a small wigwam made by her mother. She went on a fast and was instructed not to touch her body or face—she had to use a stick if she needed to scratch herself. After four days, she returned to her family, and a feast was held in her honor. During menstruation, it was believed that powerful spirits were present in a woman's life, and she could harm herself or others in the band. Throughout her life, a woman had to remove herself from daily tasks whenever she had her period.

When a boy killed his first game, a feast was held in his honor. People gave thanks and prayed that the boy would continue on the path to becoming a great hunter. Of course, the first kill wasn't always a bear. One Ojibwe man, Henry Selrick, recalled that as a boy he killed a wild canary. He hung up his "first kill" until he had hunted enough game for a proper feast, but by that time the little bird had become completely shriveled.

When he came of age, a boy went on a vision quest to seek his guardian spirit and to determine what he would become in life. His father took him into the woods, made him a shelter or a nest in a tree, then left him there for several days. Alone in the woods, the boy fasted and dreamed—usually for four days. The father returned from time to time to check on his son. A boy might have to embark on several quests before he found his guardian spirit and a dream revealed his future.

Marriage. The Ojibwe used many talismans in hopes of influencing the future. Among them was a love charm, often the wooden figures of a man and a woman tied together. Tucked into a small bag, along with a piece of the beloved's clothing and some love medicine concocted from seeds and herbs, the love charm was carried by the person wishing to cast a spell on his or her beloved. The Ojibwe were quite romantic. One young woman once wrote, "My love is tall and graceful as the young pine waving on the hills, and swift in his course as the noble, stately deer; his hair is flowing, and dark as the blackbird that floats through the air."

Young men often played their flutes in the evening, but young women were not allowed to leave the wigwam and join them. If a young man wished to court, he had to visit her in the company of her family. If a couple wished to marry, they spoke to the parents or elders of the family. There was no formal wedding—the couple simply lived together for a year, after which the woman could return to her family if she failed to conceive a child or if the pair didn't get along. If the couple wished to stay together, they lived with the wife's family for about a year and then built their own wigwam. Divorce was permitted, as was intermarriage with Europeans, and many women wed French traders and trappers.

Death. When clan members died, they were washed and dressed in their finest clothing and jewelry. The hair was combed and braided and then the face was painted, often brown and red. It was believed that the northern lights were the torches of the dead, or dancing ghosts with similarly painted faces. With their faces painted, the deceased could then join them. The body was wrapped in a blanket and birch bark in preparation for the journey.

Carried from the wigwam, the body was buried with its feet pointing to the west—the direction of the setting sun—which was the way to the land of the spirits. A member of the family danced around the open grave, which was filled with soil as the Midé priest, the spiritual leader of the Ojibwe, conducted the funeral ceremony. Loved ones placed a clan totem and later built a small

After death, it was believed the deceased embarked on a four-day journey to the land of the spirits. Here, the departed was reunited with friends and family who had gone on before.

bark house over the grave. The same funeral rituals were performed for the dead fetus in a miscarriage; if a baby died, the mother carried the child's clothing in a cradleboard for a year.

The Ojibwe believed that the soul journeyed for four days, so food and goods were placed with the body. Arriving in the land of the spirits, a beautiful country of clear waters and abundant game, the soul of the departed was reunited with all the relatives who had died since the beginning of time. There was much rejoicing, singing, and dancing.

The family grieved for an entire year, wearing mourning clothes and carrying a spirit bundle that held a lock of the departed's hair. The widow treated the spirit bundle as her husband, placing food before it and sleeping next to it. Mourners remained unkempt, leaving their hair unbraided or even cutting the locks. Widows, in particular, wore disheveled, dull-colored clothes and seldom combed their hair.

At the end of the year, a special ceremony was held in which mourners were comforted and offered gifts. They could then end their time of grief and rejoin the daily activities of the village.

Through the Seasons

Whether hunting animals or gathering plants, the Ojibwe treated the natural world with great respect. To take a life might break the sacred circle. The sun was the father of the people, and the earth was *aki*, literally meaning "that which is sacred." All that the wilderness provided was considered a gift from the creator and was to be received with great reverence. Ojibwe life closely followed the cycle of the seasons. Every spring and summer, the

Ojibwe moved to camps near streams and rivers where the women gathered berries, acorns, wild potatoes, milkweed flowers, bulrush root, and bark from the white pine. However, they could not always depend on the seeds, berries, roots, and leaves of wild plants. Although wild rice was among their favorite and most important foods, often, because of drought or other bad weather, there simply wasn't enough to feed their families. So, the women planted gardens near their wigwams, growing corn, beans, squash, and potatoes. Ground into a coarse meal, corn was

The Ojibwe also raised corn and other crops to supplement the wild rice they harvested from the lakes in autumn. Corn was ground into a coarse meal using a stone mortar and pestle.

included in a wide variety of dishes. As for other Native Americans, corn was an important crop for the Ojibwe, although wild rice was their primary grain.

The Ojibwe were quite adept at collecting and using wild plants and garden crops in recipes and medicines. For example, they made a drink by boiling water, then flavoring the purified liquid with wintergreen, raspberry, spruce, or wild cherry twigs. To season foods bubbling in the cooking pot, they relied on dried berries, wild ginger, bearberry, and mountain mint. They also thickened and flavored soups and stews with corn silk and dried pumpkin blossoms.

Maple Sugar and Wild Rice

For centuries the Ojibwe have tapped the trunks of maple trees in their woodland home. Early in the spring, groups of families set up sugar camps, which became their home for several weeks. Working together, they drove cedar chips into the trunk then cut a gash in the bark, just above the chip. Maple sap dripped into a birch bark pouch placed beneath the gash. When the pouch was full, it was emptied into a large birch bark or moose hide trough. Here the sap was boiled down by placing hot rocks inside. It was boiled day and night until it thickened into maple syrup. After the lean winter, people enjoyed a little of the syrup, but most was boiled down further into a crumbly brown maple sugar.

Later, when they became acquainted with French traders, the sugar makers acquired iron kettles. The kettles could be placed directly over the fire, which made boiling down the sap easier. Some of the maple sugar might then be traded for European goods—blankets, rifles, or household utensils. The rest was placed in containers and stored in caches, or pits, lined with birch bark. Over the course of the year, the maple sugar was eaten with wild rice, fish, deer, bear, and moose. It was also used to flavor wild rice, vegetables, and to sweeten fruit dishes. Or it was eaten as candy or stirred into water to make a refreshing summer drink.

For hundreds of years the Ojibwe struggled through the long northern winters, as the January winds swirled over the frozen lakes and the snow deepened around their wigwams. Hunting was hard, and often the stores of dried meat, vegetables, and fruit gave out long before the spring thaw. The people prayed to *Kitche Manitou*, the Great Spirit, to give them food they could gather each autumn, year after year, so that "we endure these long winters when the duck and the deer have vanished in the white." Not long after they had sent forth their plea, a medicine man dreamed that they would discover food growing all around them—in the very waters where they fished from their canoes.

The tall, willowy grass that thrived in the marshes was simply waiting for the people to gather its nourishing seeds. Not only the Ojibwe, but the Menominee and other northern tribes soon discovered *Manoomin*, or wild rice, which means "good seed" or "good berry." Always capitalized, the word is also sometimes

Stored in clay bowls, the wild rice on the left has not yet been threshed, or "jigged," to have the hulls removed. On the right are the dark, hard kernels produced when the process is complete.

$\mathbf{A}$fter the wild rice has been gathered, the grains must be threshed. Here, a group of men and women are beating the rice to break the hulls from the kernels.

spelled *Monomin*. Only distantly related to rice, this grass grew—and still grows—in shallow lakes and at the edges of slow-moving rivers in the upper Great Lakes region of the United States and Canada. Sprouting in the spring, wild rice grows through the summer until it reaches about three to five feet above the water in August; it is generally ready to be harvested in September. Highly nutritious, wild rice provides the most protein of all the cereal grains. The French voyageurs who traded with the Ojibwe called it *folle avoine*, or fool oats. English colonists favored the Frenchmen's fool oats, which was known as blackbird oats in Connecticut and as duck rice in Texas. In other parts of North America, it was also called Indian oats, Indian rice, and marsh rice. The Ojibwe so valued Manoomin that they traded only small amounts with the Europeans, establishing the wild rice's reputation as a rare and expensive delicacy.

Every autumn, the bands gathered near marshes and lakes to harvest the watery fields of wild rice. Long essential to the Ojibwe way of life, wild rice was more than just nourishment. The harvest meant friends and relatives once again came together in the spirit of community. A sacred gift of the Great Spirit, wild rice had to be harvested and used in a respectful way. Then, the marshes and lakes would continue to be generous to the people. Traditionally, women harvested the wild rice, although the entire family was often involved in the work preparing the grains for storage and cooking.

A few weeks before the rice was ripe women paddled out onto

the lake and tied the stems into shocks, or bunches, every few feet, wrapping them in bark to protect the grain from hungry birds. When the rice ripened, the harvesters returned, working in pairs. Standing in the stern, one harvester carefully guided the canoe beside the shock of wild rice. Sitting low in the canoe, the other harvester bent the long, rice-laden stems over the bow and lightly struck them with a cedar paddle, knocking the grains into the bottom of the canoe. The wild rice that dropped into the water became the seeds for next year's crop. The wild rice would continue to ripen throughout the autumn, and the harvesters returned several times to the gathering places.

Women parched, or heated, the wild rice in kettles placed over hot coals, shaking and stirring the grains so they would dry evenly and not burn. Parching gave the rice a smoky flavor as well as darkened the grains. The boys and men then threshed, or "jigged," the wild rice to loosen the grains from their hulls. First, they poured the parched grains into a large shallow wooden bowl or a hole in the ground lined with deerskin. Then, donning soft, clean moccasins, they danced lightly on the wild rice. Another method was tapping the wild rice with a threshing stick.

To winnow, or separate, the grain from the loosened hulls, women poured the wild rice into a birch bark tray and tossed it into the air. The autumn breeze carried away the light hulls and other chaff while the heavy grains fell back into the tray. At the end of the harvest, families celebrated with a festival of thanks to

As shown in this 1946 painting Making Wild Rice *by Patrick DesJarlait, men and women work together harvesting, hulling, and storing the precious grain that has been essential to their survival.*

the Great Spirit. Wild rice was stored in skin bags or birch containers called *makuks*. It was boiled in water and eaten with berries, and often added to soups and stews.

For centuries, entire families left their summer homes to establish wild rice camps at the lakesides for the month-long harvest. This tradition continued until the 1940s when the automobile made day trips possible, and the camps faded away. Yet, today, Ojibwe families continue to harvest, parch, hull, and store wild rice in the same manner as their ancestors, who gently paddled over the water. They do not bend the tall stems of grass until the wild rice is fully ripe—or else they would incur the Great Spirit's wrath. And to insure a bountiful harvest, they still begin each season by floating sheaves of tobacco out onto the waters.

Hunting and Fishing

People used wood and bone hooks to catch fish. They also netted or speared fish from their birch bark canoes. The fish were cooked fresh, either fried or stewed. Or the fillets were hung up and dried in the sun, or frozen if caught during the winter months. Fish eggs were eaten as well, fried or boiled. The Ojibwe often spearfished at night, attracting fish with flaming torches carried at the front of a birch bark canoe. The Ojibwe reservation of Lac du Flambeau, meaning Lake of the Torch, in northern Wisconsin was given this name by early French fur trappers because of the hundreds of torch-lit canoes that sparkled over the lake at night.

This traditional fishing method came under attack in northern Wisconsin in the 1980s when the Ojibwe insisted on their treaty rights to spearfish in waters not on their reservations. After a series of legal battles, the right to spearfish in these waters was upheld by the Supreme Court. Yet to this day, the Ojibwe are harassed by resort owners and sport fishermen who resent the

The Ojibwe have long relied on birch bark canoes for hunting, fishing, and trapping, as well as for traveling among lakes and rivers. With their boat shoved up onto the shore, this family pauses during a trip through the St. Croix area of Minnesota.

traditional spearfishing. They are inaccurately and unfairly accused of harvesting too many fish from the lakes.

The Ojibwe also hunted deer, moose, bear, waterfowl, and other animals with bow and arrow. Ducks, geese, and other birds were stewed in a pot with wild rice or potatoes, while deer and moose meat was roasted, dried, or boiled. Dripping with fat, bear meat was usually boiled; the head and paws were considered a delicacy. The liver and intestines were usually fried until crisp. Bear tallow, or fat, was used as a flavoring, a remedy for rheumatism, and a moisturizer for skin and hair.

Men relied on snares and deadfalls to trap rabbits, muskrats, otters, mink, martens, and beavers for fur as well as food. The animals were either boiled and eaten, or dried for later use. Because of their large amount of fat and tender meat, beaver tails were considered a special treat.

Making Meals

Women usually prepared one large meal each day—either at midmorning or late in the afternoon. A full meal consisted of meat or fish, broth, wild rice with maple sugar, and dried berries. Using bowls and trays of birch bark, and wooden spoons and knives made of rib bones, women stewed meats in iron kettles hung over the fire. Or they brought soups to a boil in bark pots by placing heated stones in the water until the meat and vegetables were cooked. Along with wild rice, maple sugar, and the daily dish of meat or fish, the most important food was corn. Women roasted

Women were responsible for preparing the meals. In this 1890 photograph, a woman has set up her cooking pots over a small fire within a temporary shelter in a clearing in the woods.

the ears in the husks or parched kernels in hot kettles. The kernels were then dried for storage, ground into cornmeal, or boiled with meat and other vegetables. Women also made bread by kneading dough (cornmeal, water, and a small amount of salt) into round, flat loaves, which were cooked in a frying pan over the fire.

Wild rice was—and still is—prepared in several ways. Here's a favorite Ojibwe method. Start by pouring four cups of boiling water over one cup of washed wild rice and let stand for thirty minutes. Drain and add another four cups of boiling water. Repeat the procedure twice more, adding four tablespoons of salt, if desired, during the last soaking, then drain again. This will yield about four cups of cooked wild rice.

Here's another popular way to cook wild rice. Thoroughly wash four ounces of wild rice, then place in a saucepan with three cups of cold water and one-half teaspoon of salt, or three cups of chicken stock. Bring to a boil and cook for one minute, then reduce heat and simmer for about forty-five minutes. Make sure there is enough water during the cooking time; if necessary add a little more. When the rice is tender, drain and rinse in hot water.

Once you've cooked some wild rice, you might want to try the breakfast for two from northern Minnesota on the facing page.

Clothing and Jewelry

As part of their chores in the wigwam, women made all the clothing for their families. First, they tanned deerskins, turning them into leathery sheets of buckskin. These were sewn in turn

Blueberry and Wild Rice Breakfast

1 cup cooked wild rice
1/2 cup blueberries
2 teaspoons sugar
1/2 cup milk or cream
1/4 teaspoon nutmeg

Divide the wild rice and blueberries between two bowls. Sprinkle with sugar and nutmeg. Pour milk over each serving.

into dresses for their daughters and themselves, or fashioned into breechcloths, leggings, and shirts for the boys and men. Under their dresses, women often wore a woven skirt and buckskin leggings. They also made soft-soled moccasins in a distinctive style by gathering, or puckering, the seams. Women used sinew for thread, punching holes with a sharpened bone or thorn-apple spike along the edges of the piece to be sewn.

Both men and women wore fur robes—of deer, bear, and buffalo hides—during the intense cold of the winter months. Mothers often wrapped their babies in blankets and carried them on their backs when they were old enough to be taken from the cradleboard. Muskrat and rabbit pelts were used to make hats and blankets. Moccasins were either lined with fur or stuffed with cattail down to keep out the cold. Some children wore deerskin hoods with a flap that shaded their eyes. Young children were dressed in tightly fitting clothes in the belief that they should grow tall and straight.

When they came into contact with Europeans in the late 1600s, the Ojibwe traded for blankets, which the women made into capes, hooded coats, and skirts that wrapped around their waists and were fastened with belts. Occasionally, they made clothes and hats for their children from the blankets, or they fashioned small pieces into moccasin linings. Gradually, cloth replaced leather in Ojibwe clothing.

Women usually decorated shirts, dresses, and leggings with berries, claws, small bones and porcupine quills. They were especially fond of porcupine quills, which they flattened and colored, then carefully sewed onto buckskin clothing with sinew thread. When glass beads became available to them through trade in the 1700s, the Ojibwe became highly regarded for their exquisite beadwork. They have long referred to their beads as "little spirit seeds, gift of the Manitou." It is said that when a woman is beading she must have a good attitude because the beads are a gift of beauty from the spirits. The floral pattern was an especially popular motif for adorning moccasins, leggings, and aprons with

Over time, the Ojibwe adopted Western styles of dress. Here, three boys playfully pose for the camera in cloth shirts and pants during the warm summer months in the north woods.

The delicate quills of the porcupine are still used in adorning some Ojibwe clothing. However, colorful beads, which are readily available, are now favored by most women.

both beads and quills. Women also made elaborate floral designs on small objects, including baskets and bags. In recent years, they've begun to decorate their clothing with brightly colored ribbons as well.

Men—especially old men—often wore earrings made of bones, coins, or fur during the winter. Early on, men also adorned themselves with a nose ring, often large enough to hang below the mouth. They also wore brass bracelets and armbands. Young men favored bands of fur decorated with beadwork on their wrists and ankles. They wore eagle feathers as a sign of great bravery. Both men and women grew their hair long, wearing it either loose or braided. Often they would bring out a black sheen with a bit of

The soft buckskin of this change purse is enhanced by a little beadwork. Such items are greatly admired by visitors to Ojibwe country in Michigan, Wisconsin, Minnesota, and Canada.

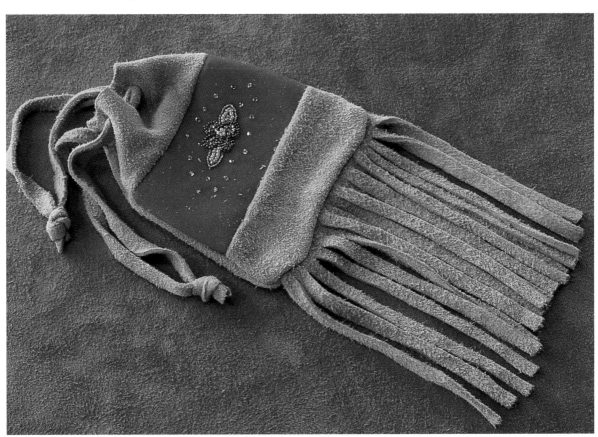

from the tree. With cords made from split tamarack or spruce roots, they sewed the pieces of bark together, then wove a cedar strip along the top edge of the canoe. To insure that the canoe was watertight, they boiled sap from the spruce tree and sealed the seams with the sticky pitch.

Although the traditional birch bark canoe has since been replaced by aluminum and fiberglass models, there is currently a resurgence of canoe making among Ojibwe men. Although the craft requires great skill and patience, many Ojibwe are again

The entire family came together to build this birch bark canoe. Working without a design, they shaped the birch bark between stakes driven into the ground, then stitched it to the wooden frame and gunnels.

designing the traditional boats, which they glide over the rice lakes in honor of their ancestors.

Games

The Ojibwe had to devote much of their time to providing food, clothing, and shelter for themselves. They did, however, also enjoy many social activities—especially visiting. They often visited friends and relatives, and enjoyed talking before and after their ceremonies. Dancing was primarily a part of religious ceremonies, but the Ojibwe enjoyed social dances too.

People also came together for two kinds of contests—games of skill and games of chance. Men particularly liked stickball—the original version of lacrosse. In this rough-and-tumble game, in which there were frequent injuries, contestants tried to fling a small ball, with the help of a racquet, through the other team's goal. The game had a religious tone—the men competed in honor of their guardian spirits. Women played a similar game with straight notched sticks and a double-ball, two balls connected with a leather thong.

Men also wrestled, competed in archery, and played snow-snake, in which contestants threw a stick as far as possible across the surface of the snow. The Ojibwe loved gambling as well, especially the moccasin game and tossing bone dice in a wooden bowl. To play the moccasin game, four bullets, one of which was marked, were hidden under four moccasins. There were usually four players on each team. The object of the game was to guess dered among the trees, admiring the tender green plants and spring flowers. He longed to know how the herbs, berries, and roots grew wild, without any help from people. He also wondered why many plants could be eaten and others made into medicine, while some were deadly poison.

Weary with hunger, Wunzh returned to his lodge and rested. He thought, "We owe our lives to the Great Spirit who created us. But could he not make it less difficult to get our food than hunting animals and gathering fruits and berries?"

The next day he was faint from his fast and remained in bed. While he was laying inside his lodge, he caught sight of a handsome young man dressed in bright colors. "The Great Spirit sent me to instruct you," the young man stated as he approached the lodge. He told Wunzh to rise and wrestle with him. Although still weak from hunger, courage rose in his heart, and the young man did as he was asked.

Just as Wunzh was about to collapse from exhaustion, the handsome young man said, "We have fought enough for one day. I will come again tomorrow." And the young man, who turned out to be a spirit being, ascended into the sky.

The next day the young man returned and renewed his struggle with Wunzh, who fought valiantly. Even as his body weakened, his mind was strengthened. Noting his great courage, the handsome young man told Wunzh, "Tomorrow will be your last trial. Be strong, my friend, for this is the only way you can overcome me and have your wish fulfilled."

Poor Wunzh was very weak in body, but through a great effort of will he refused to give up. The next day the young man returned and wrestled Wunzh again. After a long effort, the young man broke away and declared, "You have defeated me."

Sitting down with Wunzh in the lodge, the young man said, "You have wrestled with me manfully. The Great Spirit will now grant your wish. Tomorrow will be the seventh day of your fast. Your father will give you food to strengthen you. I will then wrestle one last time with you. As soon as you've prevailed over me, you must strip off my clothes and throw me on the ground. Clean the earth of roots and weeds, then soften it, and bury me there. Thereafter, come once a month and cover me with fresh earth. "

Wunzh did as he was asked. Throughout the spring he went to the grave of his friend and carefully removed the weeds and grass. He kept the earth soft as tender shoots appeared. The days and weeks of summer passed by, and Wunzh finally invited his father to the lonely place of his long fast.

A tall and graceful plant, with bright yellow silken hair, now stood upon the grave of the sky visitor. Upon the stalk grew ears of corn, or *mandaamin*, which means spirit grain. "It is my friend— the friend of all people," declared Wunzh. "We no longer need to rely on hunting and gathering alone, as long as we carefully look after this gift of the sky visitor."

Corn was thus given to the world, thanks to the good son of a poor man, to nourish people everywhere, season after season.

4.Beliefs

Made from the metal lids of snuff cans, jingles are sewn onto the long dresses of dancers. The jingles sound like bells, as the dancers stomp rhythmically to the singing and drumbeats at powwows.

ACCORDING TO OJIBWE TRADITION, THE CREATOR KITCHE MANITOU made the world in several stages. He first created rocks, water, fire, and wind. From these four elements he next made the sun, earth, moon, and the stars. During the third period, plants began to thrust up from the ground. Finally, the animals and the original people were brought forth. Because they were the first people on Earth, the Ojibwe have always felt a great need to care for the earth and to live in harmony with its plants and animals.

In addition to Kitche Manitou, there were the spirits of the four directions: North, South, East, and West. Animal spirits lived under these four manitous. The Ojibwe also believed that many other manitous, or spirits, were present in all the animals and objects in nature. Thunder, lightning, and thunderbirds were of great importance, as was the guardian spirit acquired in one's vision quest. But there were evil spirits as well—ghosts, witches, the Water Monster, and Windigo, a giant cannibal who stalked and devoured people in the woods during the long winter. Religion was deeply personal, and dreams were often interpreted as messages from the spirits.

The spirits had to be thanked and honored through prayers and offerings of tobacco and food, often through the shaman. Tobacco was so sacred that a pinch left on a tree stump could turn away a dangerous storm. Most ceremonies began with a pipe and a prayer, the smoke rising up to please the spirits. Tobacco usually accompanied an invitation to a feast or a war party. The sacred plant was also sprinkled on the water before the wild rice harvest.

The Grand Medicine Society

Among the Ojibwe, there were special ceremonies throughout the course of one's life—the naming at birth, the vision quest, marriage, and death. People also made offerings of tobacco to the rhythmic beating of drums and danced in preparation for war. The highest religious calling, however, was the healing of injuries and curing of illnesses. The Ojibwe believe that the sick and injured must be healed in body and spirit. For healing, they have long relied on herbs gathered by members of the Grand Medicine Society.

Over time, the practices of the Grand Medicine Society, or *Midéwiwin*, came to be at the heart of Ojibwe beliefs. Their teachings inscribed on birch bark rolls, this secret religious society was devoted to the spirits—especially Kitche Manitou—and dedicated to guarding the knowledge of medicine. Both men and women could become members, as long as they were respected as honest and honorable people in the community. To become members of the Midéwiwin, they underwent several days of intensive instruction followed by an initiation ceremony. Before a meeting, the members entered a sweat lodge to purify themselves. Dipping bunches of wet grass in water, they sprinkled the heated rocks until the steam wafted around them.

There were eight ranks of the Midéwiwin, the highest of which was the Great Medicine Spirit. There were songs and drums for each of the levels, and the members painted their faces to indicate which they had achieved. Made of the skin of a rattlesnake, owl,

Accompanied by songs and drumbeats, members of the Grand Medicine Society strove to gain wisdom and experience in healing both the spiritual and physical ills of their band.

weasel, or other wild creature, the Midé bag, or medicine bag, was a member's most valued belonging. It held the herbs and charms, as well as sacred white shells, that were used in healing rituals. A medicine man or woman in the society had to achieve at least the fourth level of experience and knowledge, before he or she was allowed to attend to the sick or injured.

To this day, family members bring the sick or injured person to the Midéwiwin lodge. One of the medicine men or women is then called upon to treat the patient. He or she smokes tobacco offered by the relatives, then burns sage, or perhaps cedar, to purify the air around them. Entering into a vivid dream, during which there must be absolute silence, he or she calls forth the spirits for approval of the chosen treatment. Drawing upon the strength of the Midéwiwin, the member also gives voice to songs and administers remedies to the patient from the Midé bag.

Ceremonies and Dances

In addition to the traditional ceremonies and dances, there was a war dance when men went into battle against their enemies. Upon their return, a victory dance was held. Among the social events was a begging dance in which people went from wigwam to wigwam, begging food for a feast. People also made tobacco offerings to give thanks or seek favors of the spirits. For example, they burned a little tobacco to ward off storms and to protect themselves on long and dangerous journeys.

*T*oday, the Ojibwe still carry on time-honored traditions at powwows. These events help young and old alike maintain their identity as native people. Here, a boy prepares himself for a dance competition.

Today, like many other Native Americans across the United States and Canada, the Ojibwe come together each year to strengthen their traditions. These gatherings, called powwows, feature dancers and drum groups in a variety of competitions.

*W*rapped in shawls, with their hair carefully braided, these girls are enjoying the annual powwow at Mille Lacs, Minnesota, as they await their turn in the dance competition.

There is a Grand Entry in which the American, state, and tribal flags are carried into the circle. Dignitaries and participants then dance clockwise around the circle. Accompanied by drum music and songs, the dancers then perform in different categories,

including men's traditional dance, men's grass dance, men's fancy dance, women's fancy shawl dance, jingle dress dance, and inter-tribal dance.

Of all the powwow dances, the jingle dress dance is the most recent addition—and perhaps the most distinctive. Dresses are adorned with bell-like jingles made from the lids of snuff and chewing tobacco containers. The colorful dresses are accented with a belt, purse, fan, leggings, and moccasins. The style of the dance is quite dignified, with young women standing straight and making precise, formal steps. Inspired by a dream, the jingle dance originated among the Ojibwe, possibly at Mille Lacs in Minnesota, around 1919. By the late 1920s, spreading westward into the Dakotas and Montana, the jingle dress dance had caught on among the Sioux. Today, it is a favorite dance at many powwows.

For most of this century, the jingle dance has been one of the most popular dances in competitions held throughout the Great Lakes and central Plains region. At left, girls in jingle dresses take part in the dance at Mille Lacs, Minnesota.

5. Changing World

From the time of their first contact with Europeans, the Ojibwe began to acquire new goods. They especially prized cloth, which they incorporated into their traditional dress.

Here are some examples to help with pronunciation:

a	as in **a**bout	
aa	as in f**a**ther	
e	as in caf**é**	
i	as in p**i**n	
ii	as in s**ee**n	
o	as in **o**bey	
oo	as in b**oo**t	

Vowels are nasalized if followed by **nh**, **ns**, **nz**, and **nzh**. Consonants are generally spoken as in English.

Here are some everyday words used by the Ojibwe. They may help you to better understand their culture.

beaver	amik
birch bark	wiigwaas
birch tree	wiigwaasi-mitig
boy	gwiiwizens
brother (older)	nisayenh
brother (younger)	nishiime
cat	gaazhagens
child	abinoojiinh
corn	mandaamin
cradleboard	dikinaagan
creek	ziibiins
deer	waawaashkeshi

dog	animosh
earth	aki
father	imbaabaa
fish	giigoonh
frog	omakakii
girl	ikwezens
hello	aaniin
home	endaad
house	waakaa'igan
lake	zaaga'igan
maple	aninaatig
maple sugar	ziinzibaakwad
mother	nimaamaa
mountain	wajiw
no	gaawiin
rabbit	waabooz
river	ziibi
school	gikinoo'amaadiiwigamig
sister (older)	nimisenh
sister (younger)	nishiime
snow	goon
sun	giizis
water	nibi
wild rice	Manoomin
yes	en'

6. New Ways

Many Ojibwe still embrace a traditional way of life. Here, two girls have tucked their doll into a cradleboard near Onamia, Minnesota.

Today, children may plan for careers as teachers, doctors, engineers, and other professions. Yet they also learn about their traditional culture, including the Ojibwe language, at home and at school.

many to assert their identity as native people and to seek their traditional roots.

Since the 1970s many reservations have started or supported small businesses, including campgrounds, bait shops, marinas, restaurants, service stations, hotels, fish hatcheries, and manufacturing. Today, many Ojibwe continue to live off the land by hunting, fishing, and gathering. With the passage of the Indian Gaming Regulation Act in 1988, many groups have also established casinos. Although some people oppose gambling, the revenues have brought greater employment and higher levels of income. Bands have wisely invested the income from the casinos in the purchase of ancestral lands, the establishment of businesses, the construction of homes, schools, and roads, as well as the support of health and social services. For instance, the Lac Courte Oreilles Band now cultivates a cranberry marsh, and owns a sawmill and a power plant. The Mille Lacs Band owns and operates a popular casino that supports their schools, health center, and their government, including a tribal police department.

Tribal colleges have also been established at Bay Mills in Michigan, Fond du Lac in Minnesota, Lac Courte Oreilles in Wisconsin, Rocky Boy in Montana, and Turtle Mountain in North Dakota. The Ojibwe language, once denounced by missionaries and teachers in government schools, is now taught in many communities. The Ojibwe continue to fight for lands and rights as a native people. Nearly four hundred years after first meeting French explorers, they have come to once again embrace the customs, handicrafts, and language that were gradually abandoned. The legacy of Ojibwe culture and heritage has been rekindled and is today influencing the lives of many women, children, and men— along with their deep love for the land. As Ojibwe John Rogers recalled, "Nothing the white man could teach me would take the place of what I was learning from the forest, the lakes and the river. . . . I could gain knowledge from my daily walks under the trees where the shadows mixed with the shifting sunlight and the wind fanned my cheeks with gentle caress or made me bend, as it did the trees, to its mighty blasts."

More About

Time Line

1622 The Ojibwe encounter Étienne Brulé, a Frenchman working for Samuel de Champlain in search of a passage to the Pacific Ocean, at Bowating, now known as Saint Marys River.

1679 Grand Portage Trading Post is established, and the Ojibwe begin to trade with the French.

1736–1770s The Ojibwe engage in a series of wars with the Dakotas.

1754–1760 To protect their trading interests, the Ojibwe ally with the French instead of the British in a series of wars, including King William's War (1689–1697), Queen Anne's War (1702–1713), King George's War (1744–1748), and the French and Indian War (1754–1763), collectively known in North America as the French and Indian Wars.

1830 Many Ojibwe move to Canada when the Indian Removal Act is passed. Others negotiate to remain on their lands in Michigan, Wisconsin, and Minnesota.

1837 Ojibwe forced to cede lands in Michigan, Wisconsin, and Minnesota. Michigan becomes a state.

1848 Wisconsin becomes a state.

1854–1855 In two treaties the Ojibwe cede additional lands and are forced onto reservations.

1858 Minnesota becomes a state.

1867 White Earth Reservation is established, and more land is made available to settlers.

1887 The General Allotment Act eliminates reservations.

1924 Native peoples, including the Ojibwe, are recognized as United States citizens.

1934 The Indian Reorganization Act ends allotment and recognizes rights of Native Americans.

1950s–1960s Indian rights movement leads to public protests for better living conditions for native peoples in Canada and the United States.

1968 Three Ojibwes, Dennis Banks, George Mitchell, and Clyde Bellecourt, establish the American Indian Movement (AIM) in Minneapolis, Minnesota. The group works to restore Native American rights and recover lands.

1972 The Indian Education Act provides funds for the education of Native Americans.

1978 The Indian Religious Freedom Act insures the rights of Native Americans to practice traditional religions.

1988 Following the passage of the Indian Gaming Regulation Act, the Ojibwe exercise their right to establish casinos on their reservations in the United States.

Notable People

Dennis Banks (1932–   ), a Native American activist, was born on the Leech Lake Reservation in northern Minnesota. In 1968, Banks was one of the founders of the American Indian Movement (AIM). Formed in Minneapolis, the group initially protested police practices toward Native Americans. Banks took part in protests in Denver, Colorado, and Washington, D.C. In 1973, he led the occupation of the small village of Wounded Knee on the Pine Ridge Sioux Reservation in South Dakota. For seventy-one days, Banks and other protesters defied federal officials and publicized the cause of Native American rights.

After the occupation, Banks and fellow leader Russell Means were charged with assault, larceny, and conspiracy, but the charges were dismissed.

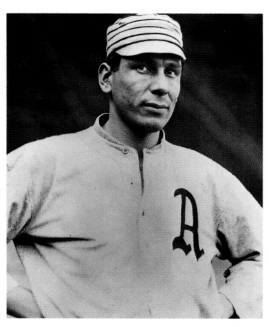

Charles Albert Bender

Charles Albert Bender (1883–1954), a renowned baseball pitcher, was born in the Bad River Band of Chippewas near Brainerd, Minnesota. He attended Carlisle Indian School and earned a college degree at Dickinson College. In 1903, he joined the Philadelphia Athletics, pitching for a team that won five American League pennants and three World Series under manager Connie Mack in a twelve-year period. In 1910, 1911, and 1914, Bender led the league in strikeouts. During his professional career, Bender won two hundred baseball games. In later years, he was a baseball coach for the U.S. Naval

Academy, the Chicago White Sox, and his old team—the Athletics. In 1953, he was elected to the National Baseball Hall of Fame.

Kimberly M. Blaeser (1915–), a poet, writer, English professor, and literary scholar, grew up on the White Earth Reservation in Minnesota. She earned a doctorate in English at the University of Notre Dame in Indiana. Her poetry has appeared in numerous literary magazines, including *Loonfeather* and *Ake:kon Journal*, and in anthologies, such as *Durable Breath* (Salmon Run Press, 1994), *Returning the Gift* (University of Arizona Press, 1994), and *The Colour of Resistance* (Sister Vision Press, 1994). Her first book of poetry was *Trailing You* (Greenfield Review Press, 1994). She has also published *Gerald Vizenor: Writing in the Oral Tradition,* which is based on her doctoral dissertation. She has published numerous articles about Native American literature and her short stories have appeared in various journals and anthologies. She presently teaches comparative literature at the University of Wisconsin-Milwaukee.

George Copway

George Copway (Kahgegwagebow) (1818–1863), a missionary and writer, was born near the mouth of the Trent River in Ontario, Canada. Although his father was a respected leader and medicine man, Copway often went hungry as a boy. Converting to Methodism in 1830, Copway worked as a missionary among his people, and then attended an academy in Jacksonville, Illinois, for two years. He became a Methodist minister in 1834. He lived in Toronto where he married Elizabeth Howell, and then in New York City where he translated several religious books from English into Algonquian language. He became a writer and lectured widely in the United States and Europe.

His many books include *The Life, History, and Travels of Kah-Ge-Ga-Gah-Bowh* (1847, reprinted as *Recollections of a Forest Life: The Traditional History and Characteristic Sketches of the Ojibway Nation* in 1850, and then as *Indian Life and Indian History* in 1858); *The Ojibway Conquest* (1850); *The Organization of a New Indian Territory East of the Missouri River* (1850); and *Running Sketches of Men and Places in England, Germany, Belgium, and Scotland* (1851). Copway later returned to his people to work again as a missionary.

Curling Hair (Curly Head, Babisigandibe, Babaseekeendase) (about 1750–1825), an Ojibwe leader, was born and raised along the southern shore of Lake Superior. About 1800, he moved to the upper Mississippi in what is now Minnesota. A chief of the Sandy Lake band, he, Noka, and Flat Mouth, other Ojibwe leaders, fought the Sioux for control of the region. He also protected trading posts, and in exchange for his support, fur traders presented him with many gifts. In turn, he welcomed the traders into his lodge and shared meat and other provisions. An expedition headed by Zebulon Pike visited him in 1805 and Curling Hair took part in a peace conference at Prairie du Chien, Wisconsin, in 1825. During the trip home he died and was succeeded by Hole-in-the-Day.

Enmegahbowh (John Johnson) (died about 1900), missionary and interpreter, was born an Ottawa in Canada, but was adopted by the Ojibwes. Educated at a Methodist school in Jacksonville, Illinois, he was ordained as Reverend John Johnson. His native name meant "he who stands among the people."

He was a Methodist missionary to the Ojibwe in Minnesota from 1839 to 1844. When the Methodists closed the mission, Enmegahbowh encouraged the Episcopal Church to establish a mission at Gull Lake, Minnesota, in 1852. Serving as an interpreter and assistant, he became an Episcopal minister there in 1858. After the Sioux Uprising of 1862–63, Enmegahbowh was the only missionary still in the region. The Gull Lake mission was relocated to the White Earth Reservation in 1869, and Enmegahbowh assisted in starting a school to train Indian clergy there in 1873.

Enmegahbowh (John Johnson)

Louise Erdrich (1954–   ), noted author, has written several best-selling novels and books of poetry. Most of her work describes the struggles of the Ojibwe and Native Americans with reservation life in North Dakota in the early years of the twentieth century. Her novels include *Love Medicine* (1984), *The Beet Queen* (1986), *Tracks* (1988), *The Crown of Columbus* (1991), and *The Bingo Palace* (1994). All of the novels, except *The Crown of Columbus*, follow the lives of an Indian family over four generations. Erdrich's books of poetry include *Jacklight* (1984) and *Baptism of Desire* (1989). She has also published short stories and articles in a number of newspapers and magazines.

Flat Mouth (1774–about 1860), a highly regarded Ojibwe leader, was the son of Wasonaunequa, a medicine man who became a chief of the Leech Lake Chippewa in Minnesota.

Like Noka, Curling Hair, and Hole-in-the-Day, Flat Mouth led Ojibwe warriors into a battle against the Sioux to gain dominance of the upper Mississippi in present-day Minnesota. Flat Mouth's people suffered many losses during this long-standing conflict, but, joined by Ojibwe from other villages, he ultimately drove the Sioux from the region. The Ojibwe still live in these areas of Minnesota that they consider their ancestral homeland.

Hole-in-the-Day (Bugonegijig), Elder (active 1812–1846), Ojibwe war chief, was also known as Hole-in-the-Sky, allied with the United States during the War of 1812 in order to receive guns. Having guns gave Hole-in-the-Day the advantage when he attacked and massacred Sioux mission camps along the Chippewa River in Minnesota. He was ambushed by Sioux warriors on his way back from a visit to Fort Snelling, but he exchanged some of his clothing and ornaments for his freedom. Hole-in-the-Day and the Ojibwe eventually drove the Sioux across the Mississippi River and out of present-day Minnesota. To end the skirmishes and raids, the U.S. Army finally established a boundary between the two tribes. Upon his death, Hole-in-the-Day was succeeded by his son of the same name.

Hole-in-the-Day (Bugonegijig), Younger (1825–1868), Ojibwe leader, was born in the same year that his father became a war chief. When his father died in 1846, Hole-in-the-Day became chief and defended Ojibwe homelands in Minnesota against raids by their traditional enemies—the Sioux. He traveled to Washington, D.C., on several occasions to negotiate with the federal government on behalf of his people. During one visit, he married a newspaper reporter, who became one of his eight wives. He was accused of making deals with the government to enrich himself at the expense of his own people. At the time of the Minnesota Uprising of the Santee Sioux, he was suspected of planning a similar rebellion by the Ojibwe. When his people were ordered to the White Earth Reservation, he refused, but then relented, and his band settled there in 1868. Shortly thereafter, he was killed at Crow Wing, Minnesota, by his own people for having betrayed them in the treaty negotiations.

Hole-in-the-Day, Younger

Peter Jones (1802–1856), a missionary, leader, and writer, was the son of a Welshman named Augustus Jones (who was a friend of the great Mohawk leader Joseph Brant) and Tuhbenahneeguay who was the daughter of the Ojibwe chief Wahbonosay. Raised in the traditional way of life, Peter was baptized and began to study religion when he was sixteen. In 1823, he and his brother John were converted at a Methodist mission near Rice Lake in Ontario, Canada. In 1826, he journeyed through Ontario, helping to convert John Sunday, George Copway, and others to the Methodist faith. During this time, he also translated religious texts into Algonquian languages. In 1830, he became a minister in the Wesleyan Methodist Church and continued to travel both as a missionary and an Ojibwe chief. He went to Toronto, New York, London, and other cities, and also worked for tribal land rights. He was the author of *The Life and Journals of Kah-ke-wa-quona-by* (1860) and *A History of the Ojibway Indians* (1861). He married an Englishwoman with whom he had four children.

Matonabbee (about 1736–1782), a Native American guide, was born near Fort Prince of Wales at the mouth of the Churchill River on the western shore of Hudson Bay in Canada. When his father died he was adopted and raised by Richard Norton, governor of the Hudson's Bay Company at the fort. When Norton returned to England, Matonabbee went to live with the hunting band of his relatives who wandered the Barren Grounds in present-day northern Manitoba, northern Saskatchewan, and the eastern Northwest Territories. During this time, he became knowledgeable and skilled in the Ojibwe way of life. Returning to the fort when he was sixteen, Matonabbee became a hunter for the British and accompanied traders on journeys along the western shore of Hudson Bay. Learning the Algonquian language of the Cree, who lived to the south, he became a negotiator among warring tribes and a chief among his people. He is best known as the guide who led Samuel Hearne of the Hudson's Bay Company on three expeditions, seeking a passage to the Pacific Ocean and copper in northern Canada. In 1782, in despair when many in his family died from smallpox, Matonabbee hanged himself.

Leopold Pokagon (Pocagin, Rib) (about 1775–1841), a leader, was born an Ojibwe, but was captured and brought up by Potawatomis in present-day Michigan. When he was a young man he was converted to Catholicism by Jesuit missionaries. After he became a chief, he asked for a priest to live in his village along the St. Joseph River near the present-day borders of Michigan and Indiana, and Father Stephen Badin moved there. Pokagon strove to keep his people from fighting in Tecumseh's legendary uprising and, twenty years later, he refused to take part in the Black Hawk War. He is best known for selling the site of Chicago to the United States in 1832 as part of the Treaty of Tippecanoe. Although he wished to live peacefully with the settlers in the region, he was forced to move his village to Dowagiac, Michigan.

Rocky Boy (Stone Child) (1860–1914) was the leader of an Ojibwe band of about 350 people that split off from their people in Wisconsin to hunt in Montana. Left out of all treaties with the United States and Canada, they avoided moving to any reservation. As more land was settled, they were unable to continue their nomadic way of life and eventually had to beg for food. Rocky Boy rose as a leader as the situation of his people became increasingly desperate. He lobbied vigorously with the Bureau of Indian Affairs for several years until "Rocky Boy's Band," as his people came to be known, were awarded a tract of land on the Fort Assinoboin military reserve in Montana. His people received the land in 1914–the same year that Rocky Boy died.

Rocky Boy

Jane Johnston Schoolcraft (1800–1841), poet and interpreter, was the daughter of a Scots-Irish fur trader and an Ojibwe woman from Sault Sainte Marie. From her mother she learned the Ojibwe language, history, and customs, including oral traditions. From her father she became acquainted with Western literature and history. As a girl, Jane began to write poetry. She often accompanied her father on trips to Detroit and Montreal. She also joined him in Ireland where she attended

Jane Schoolcraft

school from 1809 to 1810. Jane married Henry Rowe Schoolcraft, an Indian agent and friend of their family in 1823.

Under a pseudonym, Jane published several poems about Ojibwe culture, nature, and religious faith. Acting as an interpreter and informant, she also assisted her husband in his classic work as a researcher and writer about Native American culture. Devastated by the death of two of her children, Jane's health deteriorated. In 1838, her husband brought her and their other two children to New York City in hopes that Jane's health would improve. However, shortly after he departed for England, she died. Today, she is remembered for her insight into Ojibwe culture and her invaluable service to her husband.

Shingabawassin (Shingaba W'Ossin, Image Stone) (died about 1832) lived in the upper peninsula of present-day Michigan, where he warred against the Fox and the Sioux. By the early 1800s, he had become one of the most prominent chiefs among the Ojibwe.

His daughter married a trader from Montreal, and Shingabawassin became a negotiator with the traders and settlers who were moving into the region. He signed a treaty at Sault Sainte Marie in 1820, and at meetings with federal officials—including Henry Rowe Schoolcraft—he served as the main spokesperson for the Ojibwe. In a gesture of friendship, Shingabawassin pointed out the location of copper deposits at the mouth of the Ontonagon River to the newcomers.

John Tebbel (1912–   ), journalist and author, was born in Boyne City, Michigan. He earned a bachelor's degree at Central Michigan University in 1935 and a master's degree in journalism from Columbia University in 1937. He worked as a journalist for the *Detroit Free Press*, the *New York Times*, and *Newsweek*, then joined the faculty at Columbia University in 1943. Later, Tebbel chaired the journalism department at New York University from 1954 to 1964, then continued to teach journalism there. Tebbel is the author of *The American Indian Wars* (1960). He also writes about the history of journalism and contributes articles to national magazines.

Gerald Vizenor (1934–   ), author and professor, was born and raised in Minneapolis, Minnesota. After serving in the U.S. Army from 1952 to 1955, he became a guidance director for the Minnesota Department of Corrections. His early poems appeared in many books, including *Summer in the Spring: Anishinabe Lyric Poems and Stories* (1965) and *New Voices for the People Named the Chippewa* (1967). He is now professor of Native American literature in the ethnic studies department at the University of California at Berkeley.

Gerald Vizenor

Vizenor's many books of fiction include *Heirs of Columbus* (1992), *Landfill Meditation* (1991), *Griever: An American Monkey King in China* (which won a National Book Award), and *Dead Voices: Natural Agonies in the New World* (1994). He has also written nonfiction books and an autobiography entitled *Interior Landscapes* (1990).

William Whipple Warren (1825–1853), interpreter, writer, and legislator, was born at La Pointe, Wisconsin. His English father, Lyman Warren, was a blacksmith, fur trader, and Indian agent—as well as a descendant of one of the Pilgrims who came to America on the Mayflower. His mother, Mary Cadotte, was Ojibwe and French. Educated at various eastern schools, Warren became fluent in English, but he was also knowledgeable and skilled in the language and customs of the Ojibwe. He met frequently with tribal leaders and served as an interpreter for government officials. In 1850, he was elected to the territorial legislature representing his home of Crow Wing, Minnesota. He also wrote a history of his people, but was unable to get the book published. He was hoping to write two other books about the Ojibwe when he died of tuberculosis at the age of twenty-eight. His book, entitled *History of the Ojibways, Based upon Traditions and Oral Statements*, was finally published in 1885— more than three decades after his death.

William W. Warren

Glossary

Algonquian Group, or family, of over twenty languages that are the most widespread and commonly spoken in North America. Many Native American tribes speak Algonquian languages, including the Arapaho, Cheyenne, Blackfoot, Fox, Shawnee, Abenaki, and Delaware

birch bark Thin layer of bark that may be fashioned into coverings for canoes, wigwams, and household items

breechcloth A cloth or skin worn around the hips; also breechclout

buckskin Deer hide softened by a tanning or curing process

clan A number of families related to a common ancestor

Dakota Sioux people who live in the present state of Minnesota and often warred with the Ojibwe

Hiawatha A great Mohawk statesman, who helped found the League of the Iroquois; often confused with Nanabozho

lacrosse Modern sport based upon a popular stickball game of Native Americans living in the forests of eastern North America

Midéwiwin A group of medicine men and women responsible for healing and religious ceremonies. Also called the Grand Medicine Society

powwow A modern Native American gathering featuring dancers and drum groups

reservation Land set aside by the United States or Canadian governments as a home for an Indian tribe; called a reserve in Canada

wigwam A domed house made of a bent branch frame covered with birch bark

Further Information

Readings

Many fine books have been written about the six tribes that make up the Ojibwe people. Among them, the following titles were very helpful in researching and writing this book.

Danziger, Edmund Jefferson Jr. *The Chippewas of Lake Superior*. Norman, OK: University of Oklahoma Press, 1979.

Densmore, Frances. *Chippewa Customs*. St. Paul: Minnesota Historical Society Press, 1979.

Encyclopedia of North American Indians. Tarrytown, NY: Marshall Cavendish, 1997.

Hilger, M. Inez. *Chippewa Child Life and Its Cultural Background*. St. Paul: Minnesota Historical Society Press, 1951, 1992.

Hodge, Frederick Web, ed. *Handbook of American Indians North of Mexico*. New York: Rowman and Littlefield, 1965.

Johnston, Basil. *Ojibway Ceremonies*. Lincoln: University of Nebraska Press, 1982.

Kohl, J. G. *Kitchi-Gami: Life Among the Lake Superior Ojibway*. St. Paul: Minnesota Historical Society Press, 1985.

Landes, Ruth. *The Ojibwa Woman*. Lincoln: University of Nebraska Press, 1938, 1997.

Langer, Howard J., ed. *American Indian Quotations*. Westport, CT: Greenwood Press, 1996.

Malinowski, Sharon, and Anna Sheets. *The Gale Encyclopedia of Native American Tribes*. Detroit: Gale Research, 1998.

Malinowski, Sharon. *Notable Native Americans*. Detroit: Gale Research, 1995.

Shanks, Ralph, and Lisa Woo Shanks. *The North American Indian Travel Guide.* Petaluma, CA: Costano Books, 1993.

Trigger, Bruce G. *Handbook of North American Indians. Northeast.* Volume 15. Washington, DC: Smithsonian Institution, 1978.

Vennum, Thomas. *Wild Rice and the Ojibway People.* Minnesota Historical Society Press, 1988.

Waldman, Carl. *Who Was Who in Native American History: Indians and Non-Indians from Early Contacts Through 1900.* New York: Facts on File, 1990.

Young people who wish to read more about the Ojibwe will enjoy these excellent books for children, a number of which were also consulted in researching and writing *The Ojibwe*:

King, Sandra. *Shannon: An Ojibway Dancer.* Minneapolis: Lerner Publications, 1993.

Lund, Bill. *The Ojibwa Indians.* Mankato, MN: Bridgestone Books, 1997.

Lunge-Larsen, Lise. *The Legend of the Lady's Slipper: An Ojibwe Tale.* Boston: Houghton Mifflin, 1999.

McLellan, Joseph. *Nanabosho & Kitchie Odjig.* Winnipeg: Pemmican Publications, 1997.

Norman, Howard A. *Trickster and the Fainting Birds.* San Diego, CA: Harcourt Brace, 1998.

Regguinti, Gordon. *The Sacred Harvest: Ojibway Wild Rice Gathering.* Minneapolis: Lerner Publications, 1992.

San Souci, Robert D. *Sootface: An Ojibwa Cinderella Story.* New York: Bantam Doubleday Dell Books for Young Readers, 1994.

Spooner, Michael. *Old Meshikee and the Little Crabs: An Ojibwe Story.* New York: H. Holt and Co., 1996.

Stan, Susan. *The Ojibwe.* Vero Beach, FL: Rourke Publications, 1989.

Van Laan, Nancy. *Shingebiss: An Ojibwe Legend.* New York: Houghton Mifflin, 1997.

The two stories included in this book were adapted from versions collected by Henry Rowe Schoolcraft and published in *Algic Researches, Comprising Inquiries Respecting the Mental Characterisistics of the North American Indians*, two volumes published by Harper Brothers in 1839.

The recipes in *The Ojibwe* were adapted from *Original Minnesota Ojibway (Chippewa) Indian Recipes.*

Ojibwe Organizations

Bad River Tribal Council
P. O. Box 39
Odanah, WI 54861
(715) 682-4212
Fax (715) 682-6679

Bay Mills Executive Council
Route 1
Brimley, MI 49715
(906) 248-3241
Fax (906) 248-3283

Curve Lake Indian Reserve
Whetung Ojibwa Craft Centre & Art Gallery
Curve Lake, Ontario KOL 1RO Canada
(705) 657-3661

Fond du Lac Reservation Business Committee
105 University Road
Cloquet, MN 55720
(218) 879-4593
Fax (218) 879-4164

Grand Portage Reservation Business Committee
P. O. Box 428
Grand Portage, MN 55605
(218) 475-2279
Fax (218) 475-2284

Red Cliff Tribal Council
P. O. Box 529
Bayfield, WI 54814
(715) 779-5805
Fax (715) 779-3151

Red Lake Tribal Council
P. O. Box 550
Red Lake, MN 56671
(218) 679-3341
Fax (218-679-3378

Saginaw Chippewa Tribal Council
7070 East Broadway Road
Mt. Pleasant, MI 48858
(517) 772-5700
Fax (517) 772-3508

St. Croix Council
P. O. Box 287
Hertel, WI 54845
(715) 349-2195
Fax (715) 349-5768

Sandy Lake Band of Ojibwe
HCR 3, P. O. Box 562-7
McGregor, MN 55760
(218) 839-3504

Saute Ste. Marie Chippewa Tribal Council
206 Greenough Street
Saute Ste. Marie, MI 49783
(906) 635-6050
Fax (906) 635-0741

Sokaogon Tribal Council
Route 1, P. O. Box 625
Crandon, WI 54520
(715) 478-2604
Fax (715) 478-5275

White Earth Reservation Business Committee
P. O. Box 418
White Earth, MN 56591
(218) 983-3285
Fax (218) 983-3641

Websites

American Indians have assumed great prominence on the Internet. Here is just a sampling of some of the best and most interesting websites created by or about the Ojibwe and other native peoples.

Bad River Band of Lake Superior Chippewa Indians
http://www.newnorth.net/glitc/badriv1.htm

Chippewa/Ojibway/Anishinabe Literature
http://www.indians.org/welker/chippewa.htm

Fond du Lac Band of Chippewa Indians
http://indy4.fdl.cc.mn.us/~isk/maps/mn/fondlac.htm

Grand Portage Band of Chippewa Indians
http://indy4.fdl.cc.mn.us/~isk/maps/mn/grandport.htm

Great Lakes Intertribal Council
http://www.newnorth.net/glitc/

Keweenaw Bay Indian Community (L'Anse Reservation)
http://www.ojibwa.com/

Lac du Flambeau Band of Lake Superior Chippewa
http://www.newnorth.net/glitc/ldf.htm

Michigan Indian Tribes
http://indy4.fdl.cc.mn.us/~isk/maps/mi/michigan.html

Mille Lacs Band of Chippewa Indians
http://indy4.fdl.cc.mn.us/~isk/maps/mn/millelac.htm

Mille Lacs Band of Ojibwe
http://www.millelacsojibwe.org/home2.html

Mille Lacs Indian Museum
http://www.dted.state.mn.us/ebranch/mhs/sites/mlim.html

Minnesota Indian Artists

http://indy4.fdl.cc.mn.us/~isk/art/art_minn.html

Native American Authors: Ojibwe Tribe

http://www.ipl.org/cgi/ref/native/browse.pl/t206

Ojibway Customs

http://www.turtle-island.com/customs.html

Ojibway Indian Culture

http://www.ksc.nasa.gov/external/groups/naic/ojibway.htm

Ojibways of the Pic River First Nation

http://www.picriver.com/

Ojibwe

http://kroeber.anthro.mankato.msus.edu/nativeNA/ojibwe.html

Ojibwe History

http://www.dickshovel.com/ojib.html

Ojibwe Language and Culture

http://www.citilink.com/~nancyv/ojibwe/

Sault Ste. Marie Tribe of Chippewa Indians

http://www.sootribe.org/

Turtle Island Productions

http://www.turtle-island.com/home.html

Turtle Mountain Band of Chippewa Indians

http://www.utma.com/~kferris/

Index

Page numbers for illustrations are in **boldface**.

Raymond Bial

HAS PUBLISHED OVER THIRTY CRITICALLY ACCLAIMED BOOKS OF PHOTOGRAPHS for children and adults. His photo-essays for children include *Corn Belt Harvest, Amish Home, Frontier Home, Shaker Home, The Underground Railroad, Portrait of a Farm Family, With Needle and Thread: A Book About Quilts, Mist Over the Mountains: Appalachia and Its People, Cajun Home,* and *Where Lincoln Walked.*

He is currently immersed in writing *Lifeways,* a series of books about Native Americans. As with his other work, Bial's deep feelings for his subjects is evident in both the text and illustrations. He travels to tribal cultural centers, photographing homes, artifacts, and surroundings and learning firsthand about the national lifeways of each of these peoples.

A full-time library director at a small college in Champaign, Illinois, he lives with his wife and three children in nearby Urbana.